IN THE IMAGE
of Christ

IN THE IMAGE
of Christ

ESSAYS ON BEING CATHOLIC AND FEMALE

PHYLLIS ZAGANO

IN THE IMAGE OF CHRIST
Essays on Being Catholic and Female
Phyllis Zagano

Edited by Gregory F. Augustine Pierce
Designed and typeset by Patricia A. Lynch
Cover image by Chris Sardegna. Provided by Crew Labs Inc. on Unsplash.com.
Creative Commons Zero/public domain.

Library of Congress Number: 2015948535
ISBN: 978-0-87946-548-3
Printed in the United States of America by Total Printing Systems
Year 25 24 23 22 21 20 19 18 17 16 15
Printing 10 9 8 7 6 5 4 3 2 First
♲ Text printed on 30% post-consumer recycled paper.

Contents

For Irene Kelly, RSHM

Introduction

There is always something to say about the Catholic Church, its teachings, its foibles, its influence, and its people. During the past several years I have had the privilege of writing a column from the Catholic perspective, for a few years nationally syndicated by the Religion News Service, more recently online and occasionally in print editions of the *National Catholic Reporter* and various other journals in the United States and around the world.

Column writing is a difficult art, far different from the academic writing I more usually do, although in many respects equally measured and researched. For me, the columns grow from reading the news—Catholic and otherwise—and thinking and praying about how the news impacts what I see as the basic impetus of faith: Justice. So my column is called "Just Catholic." I take no quarrel with the teachings of the faith, but I do disagree mightily with some of the disciplines overlaid on the church's history, the disciplines that ignore the needs of the people of God.

The columnist typically returns to one or a few favored topics, as world news turns the wheel again to show another side to the story. Much of my writing—academic and journalistic—is about women in ministry in the Catholic

Church. So I write about that. Another deep theme is the ways women around the world are treated, often mistreated, simply because they are female.

In my writing and in my thought I draw a straight line from the ways in which some in authority in Catholicism speak about women to the general disrespect too many women suffer in too many parts of the world. The blindness to this fact astonishes me.

On the one hand, the church rightfully says that all are made in the image and likeness of God. On the other hand, the church (or at least some parts of it) presents an argument that women cannot be sacramentally ordained because women cannot image Christ.

My academic research into the restoration of women as deacons proceeds from these truths. I do not disagree that the church believes it has definitively ruled out women in the priesthood. But, if that indeed is the case, what is the argument against women in the diaconate? I find only two points: 1) women deacons of history only ministered to women; 2) women cannot image Christ.

The second argument (women cannot image Christ) requires that the first argument (women only ministered to women) be rescued from the ash heaps of history. If women were then needed to minster to other women, how much more is women's ministry needed today, when the church seems to argue that women cannot image Christ? Jesus, the Christ, was indeed male. But the sign and symbol of every sacrament is the Risen Lord who has transcended the bonds of flesh and who lives today in the church.

The Christian vocation is to become another Christ. The simple fact of the matter is that we all image Christ. To say a woman cannot receive the sacrament of order to the rank of deacon because she is a woman is to say a woman is somehow less than human, that, like the cat or lamppost I recall in one of my columns here, she cannot image Christ.

I respectfully disagree with those who intimate that I and half the population of the planet are somehow less than human.

The few columns here printed were selected by ACTA publisher Greg Pierce, whose enthusiastic support of the project has been matched by his careful eye—and ear—and his belief in what I have tried to point out about women in the church and in the world in columns published during months and years past. Not all of my essays on women are here printed, but the carefully-selected few coherently present my case and my views. The essays are slightly edited and updated. I am grateful for the care everyone at ACTA have shown my writing.

I am grateful as well for the able assistance I have received over the years at Hofstra University on this and other projects from my research assistant, Dr. Carmela Leonforte-Plimack, from my student assistant for this project Sarah Andrea Esteban, from Department of Religion and Philosophy administrative assistant, Joanne Herlihy, and from manager of instructional design Monica Yatsyla and the students and staff of Faculty Computing Services.

While several of these essays appeared in print in various publications around the world, most first appeared in *National*

Catholic Reporter online under the careful eyes and pens of Stephanie Yeagle, Pam Cohen, and Dennis Coday. As always, I am grateful for their encouragement and assistance.

The work is dedicated to my dear friend Irene Kelly, RSHM, who served as reader for each column prior to its first publication. My sense of what the church and the world needed me to say was enhanced by her sense of how to say it.

Phyllis Zagano
Feast of St. Martha
July 29, 2015

I. IN THE IMAGE OF CHRIST

In the Image of Christ

I love the church. I love the people of God. I belong to it. I belong to them.

I do not belong to a church of good-old-boy camaraderie or to one that looks the other way when its ministers do something wrong. I know the criticisms of Catholic clergy and hierarchy today, yet I know not all priest and bishops or even popes can or should be criticized. The complaints about the church are not all that different from those about any bureaucracy. The church has grown into a multinational corporation that can rival any other, and it has its own bureaucracy to manage its affairs. (That, of course, is the church's Achilles' heel: Ministry in too many places has been replaced by bureaucracy.)

But I do not belong to the church of the bureaucrats. I belong to the church that is the People of God who have seen and heard and believe and act on the Good News proclaimed by Jesus of Nazareth, the Christ.

I think the bishops and their priests believe the Gospel. But they are increasingly tangled in the bureaucratic web that complicates their every move and reminds them there's a lawyer around every bend.

If you look down the toll road that bureaucracy says leads

to salvation, you will see that many toll booths make some sense, and some others make a lot of sense. It's just that too many church toll-takers are so bored, so angry, so heartless in their unwillingness to make any change that the road backs up and folks go over the median to someplace...anyplace...else.

But to whom shall we go? The fact is, being Catholic does not mean being a toll payer any more than it means being a toll taker. It means carrying or being carried by the Gospel in all its forms, in all its iterations. It is less about judging and more about enjoying the very precious days of life we have been given.

I know the church's hierarchy seems to have transcribed every single saying of Jesus into one law or another. But the church I belong to is not one of law any more than it is the church of bureaucracy. No, the church I belong to is the church of the prophets. It is the church of Oscar Romero and of Dorothy Day. It is the church of soup kitchens and children's shelters. It is the church that knows both women and men are made in the image and likeness of God, and that we all can, and really do, image Christ.

And Then
the Angel Left Her

Luke ends the annunciation narrative with a bang: "And then the angel left her." Mary agrees to the mystery and now is on her own. What does she feel, this young woman about to become pregnant who-knows-how? Alone.

There are what, 3.5 billion women and girls in the world? How many are alone? I don't mean without friends or family. I mean alone in their choices, in their situations, in their lives. How many look up and see, for just a moment, an angel to light the way? How many, like Mary, accept the will of God?

No life is easy.

How could Mary be so free? What fine cuts to her character prepared her to shine so? How did she manage, knowing—as we must presume–that her child would be just as the angel said: holy, the Son of God?

I'd be scared to death.

Of course, we know little about Mary beyond Scripture's testimony. From it we can assume that Mary spent a lot of time on her own, before, during, and after Jesus' birth.

As the story unwinds every Christmas, Mary is still surrounded by men. The crèche figures near the Christ child are all male. There are shepherds, not shepherdesses. There are kings, not queens. Animals, yes, and in many depictions a few angels hovering about. But following the narrative, there is no sister, no midwife, no female helper to be found.

Was the nativity an entirely male affair? Did Mary have female friends along the way to Jerusalem, or when she and poor, dear Joseph got stranded in Bethlehem? Did a midwife send Joseph out for warm water when her time came? Did a woman help her nurse the child?

Did "the girls" come round to see Mary's baby boy once the three of them got back to Nazareth? Did her mother and her sisters and her female cousins crowd into the little house to celebrate his circumcision?

Why is all this testimony about the birth of a child, about the birth of this Child, so devoid of women?

Two points here: First, there is not one woman in the annunciation or incarnation narrative besides Mary, even as the angel points to Elizabeth's pregnancy for proof of God's power; second, we can only assume that Mary sought and received the support of women, as she did when she went to see her cousin Elizabeth. But there is nothing more in Scripture.

Yes, there are women with her when her son died, but now it is Christmas, and the Christ is breaking forth into, let's face it, an all-male world. That is a silly and unnatural rendering of this most magnificent example of God's largesse. How could the God of our fathers—and our mothers—send his son to a world without women? How could the God who according to the philosophers is neither male nor female choose to be with only half the race? It makes no sense. In fact, it makes no sense at all.

Yet that is what the centuries have handed on to us today. That is how it reads in Scripture. But the God who is both mother and father to the ages and to us each and all could never be so selective.

Mary knew this. Mary knew no doubt that, even though imprisoned by her culture, she could face the truth the angel announced and bring it into the world. Her choice, her yes, her fiat, resounded then and echoes now. Her yes serves to cheer along those other women, all alone, who follow her example and who follow their own roads and paths.

There is very little we can do to unravel what may be a huge misreporting of the story, but there are many ways to encourage the women hearing it to pick up their heads and say—no, to pick up their heads and cry out—for all the world to hear: the story of woman, any woman, is not of subjugation, and it is not of fear.

The world can and should call forth its own angels to be with the women who, like Mary, have impossible tasks before them. The world must supply the graces for the women living with improbable requests made by fleeting angels who brought good and wonderful news but who, when all is said and done, left them.

It is up to the rest of us to take up wings and help those women stay the course. Then, may they and we welcome the Christ Child and, not incidentally, image him.

What Would
Mary Magdalene Do?

Once a pope trashes you, it's pretty much downhill from there. So once Pope Gregory the Great in 591 declared that the "sinful" woman in Luke's Gospel who anointed Jesus' feet was Mary Magdalene, a whole industry developed to discredit her. That's big stuff. I mean, she is the one who announced the Resurrection.

Or have they changed that, too?

I can't help but wonder what Mary Magdalene would have done if she heard—even got a copy of—old St. Gregory's homily on Luke 7:36-50 erasing all she had done, all she had said, all she had been.

How would she receive it? What pain would it cause? Would she be able to respond?

Who knows if Gregory wrote it himself? Still, it was quite obviously written by a man, for men. No matter the history of women in ministry, by the sixth century women who wished to serve the church were steered toward cloisters. And beyond an occasional queen or two, women were not well-received in the papal courts. So Mary's successors had little—if any—input to the papacy's day-to-day business. For sure, they were pretty much shut out.

So what would she have seen and heard?

Bring Mary Magdalene to Rome just as Gregory is about to preach. Picture her as she somehow snuck into the back of the church or the basilica or wherever that particular 50-year-old successor to St. Peter was speaking that day. Sit next to her and hear him say, "It is clear, brothers, that the woman previously used the unguent to perfume her flesh in forbidden acts."

Whoa! Did he say that? I always thought the perfume—the jar of nard—was all she owned. I always thought it was what she had for her own burial. I mean, it never occurred to me she used it for, shall we say, business transactions. In fact, it never occurred to me that—whether she was Mary Magdalene or not—the woman was a prostitute at all. If the current penalty for adultery or prostitution in lands not far from Magdala is death by stoning, I can't see how Luke's Mary made it through life, let alone through the door to be near Jesus.

So, yes, see Mary Magdalene sitting there, listening to the indictments read against her. Would she have recognized herself? Doubtful. Would she have been able to answer? No. Would she be troubled? You bet.

So what's her situation? She has been unfairly accused. Her actions (and probably her words) have been taken out of context. She has been publicly excoriated by the highest church authority. And she is essentially helpless.

Is she in tears? Can she sleep? How can she defend herself against lies? How can she recover from the assault, from the abuse, at the hands of that pope (and, not incidentally, his minions through the ages)?

Can we detect a pattern here?

Public excoriation seems to be a favorite indoor sport in the winding halls and storied walls where mostly clerics serve the pope. And, as if today's pope does not produce enough words on his own, there's now a traditionalist rumor afloat that every word from every Vatican congregation or commission flows directly from the pope's mind. It's as if the whole crowd of them was sitting on some funhouse Chair of Peter.

Once upon a time, Rome's message-control department only needed wax for the papal seal. Later, things got out of hand with everybody claiming papal authority, directly or indirectly. It's just plain silly. Think schoolyard children: "My boss is bigger than your boss."

There's a zinger for everyone: sisters, nuns, married women, working women. OK, not quite everyone, just the female everyones. You know the litany: the LCWR thing, the birth control thing, the "radical feminist" thing. From here, it looks like half the church has been labeled reborn Magdalenes and locked out of curial offices, with no way to respond, no way to react, no way out.

That is the sadness in the church today. It took almost a millennium and a half for Pope Paul VI, in 1969, to indirectly disconnect Mary Magdalene from the slur Gregory "the Great" levied on her.

We are all Magdalenes. How long will it take for the rest of us to be restored?

II. WOMEN DEACONS

It's Time
for Women Deacons,
Your Holiness

Your Holiness:

Forgive my presumption in addressing you directly, but the matter I bring is both urgent and pressing. Women are no longer walking away from the church. They are running away. They are running toward churches that make it clear women are made in the image and likeness of God.

I am not writing to argue for woman priests. But Cardinal Ratzinger told me many years ago in New York women deacons were "under study." From 1992-2002, the International Theological Commission worked on that question, producing a report essentially repeating what he said: the Magisterium must decide.

When Pope Benedict met with the priests of Rome in 2006, he wondered aloud: could the church open more positions of responsibility to women? Was he then signaling the recovery of the tradition of women deacons?

In 2009, Benedict changed Canon Law to echo the Catechism. Priests are ordained to act in the person of Christ, the head of the church; deacons are ordained to serve the people of God in and through the Word, the liturgy and charity. Since doctrinal statements only forbid women priests, and deacons are not priests, it seems he removed another hurdle.

You know it is not just me asking. Thousands of people sent the Congregation for the Doctrine of the Faith e-mails and postcards about women deacons in a campaign organized by the US-based group FutureChurch. Several other organizations, including the Canada-based *Femmes et Ministères*, have claimed April 29, the feast of St. Catherine of Siena, as an international day of prayer for women deacons.

It is a new-old question. The only person in scripture with the formal job title "deacon" is Phoebe, deacon of the church at Cenchreae (Romans 16:1). Some see the start of the diaconate in Jesus' washing the apostles' feet at the Last Supper, but most see it really beginning with the apostles calling the seven to a more formal ministry (Acts 6:1-6). There were many women deacons in the early church.

The bishops of the world were talking about women deacons at the Second Vatican Council. They are still at it. Most recently, the Irish bishop of Kilmore, Leo O'Reilly, said women deacons should be considered. A while back, the Swiss Bishop of St. Gall, Markus Büchel, said women deacons were a good idea. Others before them—even the Jesuit Cardinal Carlo Martini,—wanted to restore women to the diaconate. Bishops from Australia to Ireland say more women in power would have stemmed the priest sex mess. I think they are correct.

I am told your Curia knows women can be ordained as

deacons but does not want women in the clerical structure of the church. That cuts both ways, Holy Father. A lot of women do not want anything to do with clericalism. Some want the whole system to collapse. More say it has collapsed already.

Where is the church without women? I know you are concerned about the fading influence of Christianity in Europe. I write from the United States. Things are pretty bad over here, too. The country is over three-quarters Christian (with 70 million Catholics) but newspapers like *The New York Times* no longer has front page Easter stories. Their ink is used on scandal.

The Christian message is being lost in the daily drama of the sex abuse crisis. I fear, Most Holy Father, that bad priests and worse bishops will cloud your legacy. You are doing wonderful things about Vatican finances, but you still may be remembered as the pope who belatedly started a laboring sludge pump to clear the swamp.

I know you love what God loves and hate what God hates, but I also know how bureaucracy can stymie even (maybe especially) the most brilliant person. Is the bureaucracy keeping you from doing the right thing on women deacons?

Let me come to the point. The Catholic Church in developed nations is dying out. I am convinced it is dying because of the way it relates to women. Surely you see the numbers—declining membership and eroding donations—but do you have any idea how angry women are? And every woman Rome alienates extends her influence to several others—to her husband, her children, her friends, her neighbors—until the last person out the parish door closes the lights.

If I may, I think it is time for you to make a decision about women deacons.

It is an opportunity for you to state the Christian message in a way that can be heard. Yes, God is love and all persons are made in the image and likeness of God. But the world will not and cannot hear that until you have a woman deacon standing beside you, proclaiming the Gospel in St. Peter's.

Again, pardon my presumption, but perhaps no one else will tell you.

The Case
for Women Deacons

While every website mention of "women deacons" brings out the crazies, there are increasing numbers of nonprofessional commentators whose postings demonstrate serious reflection.

Still, the most violent combination of anger and misinformation I receive comes at the mention of women as deacons, and I cannot for the life of me figure out why. There is nothing spectacular about women deacons. They are a historical fact in both Catholicism and in Orthodoxy, and the effort to restore them more broadly has been gaining momentum for many years.

The Greek Orthodox theologian Evangelos Theodorou wrote about ordained women deacons in his tradition almost 60 years ago, and Elizabeth Behr-Sigal followed suit about 35 years ago. Since then, Kyriaki Karidoyanes FitzGerald has continued the discussion. My own work on Catholic women deacons follows on theirs, joined by extraordinary documentary research by Gary Macy, Carolyn Osiek, Kevin Madigan, and others.

But the question—it really is not an "issue"—raises hackles and voices from among those who respond to my articles and opinion columns. Some exclaim about camels' noses and tent flaps; others whine that any woman who thinks about becoming a deacon should become an Episcopalian. Many more deny the absolute fact that the question is open. One associate professor at a Midwestern seminary even wrote his own "letter" to the pope. He said, "Millions of women have lived their Catholic faith and have made inestimable contributions to the Church without any desire to prance about the sanctuary in clerical garb."

He really wrote that, clearly encapsulating the objections and fears of Rome, of the crazies, and of this lone professor. I honestly never thought about it, but apparently they simply cannot stomach the idea of a woman in vestments! The problem is not women as deacons, or women doing the diaconal work of the church. It is not a problem of women teaching and preaching, of marrying and baptizing, of stewardship or of management. The problem for those who mock the concept of women as deacons simply do not want to see women dressed in clerical garb.

So if my local bishop on his next *ad limina* visit to Rome mentions women deacons, the thought that springs to his mind and that of everyone in the room is a woman weighted down with tons of satin, silk, and lace? That is just plan nuts.

The concept of women as deacons is not about Sunday dress-up time. The concept of women as deacons is about service to the church, to the whole church, and especially to the women of the church too often bereft of ministry that speaks to their needs on their terms and in their words.

And the church needs the ministry of women to

rebuild it, as it suffers under the weight of all those pederasts, philanderers, embezzlers, closed schools, and parishes.

Women deacons are for ministry. It is about serving the people of God.

Visit Your Bishop

The Lord is risen! He is risen indeed! Go tell your bishop. While you're there, let him know that Jesus first appeared to a woman.

The liturgy police have done it again. They've shortened John's beautiful account of the Resurrection so that the Easter Sunday Gospel stops short of Jesus' first appearance. That would be to Mary Magdalene.

Why? Ask your bishop.

The fact of the matter is, a woman first witnessed and first proclaimed the central fact of Christianity: Christ has risen. Not only that: The men believed her. Why is it such a problem for women to proclaim that today?

It wasn't always like this. It does not need to be like this.

Oh, you say, don't use the "O" word–ordination. The law is the law. Well, let me tell you something about law. To begin with, law is not theology. The law reflects practice, which grows from theology, but the law is not theology. The law that effectively keeps women's hands off the Gospel is just that: a discipline, not a theological fact.

So when you visit your bishop, you might point that out to him in case the subject of women ordained to the diaconate comes up. Women were and can again be deacons. Deacons rightfully proclaim the Gospel. Deacons rightfully preach.

The word "deacon," you know, means "servant." Its deeper meanings bring forth "one who carries the message." That would be the hundreds of thousands of women in today's church who serve and teach and heal. They proclaim the Gospel's teachings by their lives and by their actions, sometimes using words. They are the ones whose hearts are penetrated by the message of Christ. But at Mass, they cannot read the Gospel; and at Mass, they cannot preach.

Does your bishop know why women cannot be returned to the order of deacons? Chances are he's heard the recitative:

1. Women cannot be ordained deacons because they cannot image Jesus;
2. Women cannot be ordained deacons because the law forbids it;
3. Women cannot be ordained deacons because women deacons of history only ministered to women;
4. Women cannot be ordained deacons because (get this) we don't want to upset the Orthodox.

Glory! Just as with the Gospel, they keep tweaking the facts!

First: Every sacrament is sign and symbol of the living Christ. The deacon does not represent the human male Jesus; the deacon represents Christ the servant. A woman cannot image the risen Christ? That implies women are not made in the image and likeness of God.

Second: "The law" means Canon 1024 (only a male is

validly ordained), which was developed to restrict women from priesthood. New Congregation for the Doctrine of the Faith regulations levy excommunication for women's ordination without distinguishing what is (diaconal ordination) and what is not (priestly ordination) supported by Tradition.

Third: Women can only minster to women? What do you think is going on now? The women deacons of history anointed other women–for baptism, for extreme unction, for burial. The women deacons of history catechized, prayed with, and gave spiritual direction to other women. How about we stick with Tradition and bring these forward through the ordained ministry of the church?

Fourth: We can't get ahead of the Orthodox. Hello? The Eastern churches have a deep tradition of ordained women, to modern times. The Armenian Apostolic Church has women deacons, and the holy synod of the Orthodox Church of Greece voted to restore the tradition 10 years ago. The Catholic Church accepts the sacramentality of their orders, so what about their women deacons?

I know your bishop is busy, but why not send him a note or at least give him a call? Remind him of what Pope Francis wrote in *Evangelii Gaudium*: "But we need to create still broader opportunities for a more incisive female presence in the Church."

That might get his attention.

III. WOMEN RELIGIOUS

Surrounding Clericalism
with an Octagon of Statements

In the summer of 2014, approximately 800 members of the Leadership Conference of Women Religious gathered in Nashville, Tennessee. Against a backdrop of Vatican criticism of their organization and of the sister who would receive LCWR's annual award, the sisters listened as a Vatican representative listed eight points for their reflection.

A letter from the prefect of the Congregation for Institutes of Consecrated Life and Societies of Apostolic Life–the acronym they use is CICLSAL–challenged the sisters, asking:

1. about their return to the sources of Christian life;
2. had they adapted in an evangelical way to the changed conditions of the times;
3. if their supreme rule is to follow Christ in the Gospel;
4. do they preserve their founding charisms;
5. do they "think with the church";
6. are their members made aware of the needs of the church so they may live in communion with others;
7. is each member loved personally;

8. whether obedience and authority are dimensions of the life of true fraternity amongst them or instruments of power and of enslavement, perhaps disguised by an unhealthy spirituality?

My friends, can we not surround clericalism with this octagon of statements? Can we not consider the specter of an unfeeling church bureaucracy that ignores real situations? Can we not reflect on the ways some clerics personally and institutionally treat others?

I refer here specifically to the last of the eight points I summarized above. The letter from the prefect of CICLSAL questions, directly, whether obedience and authority are measures of true fraternity. (I will skip over the fact that he read the letter to 800 women.) The CICLSAL letter directly questions whether obedience and authority are "instruments of power and enslavement, perhaps disguised by unhealthy spirituality."

That is what the suffering caused by clericalism is all about. Are obedience and authority instruments of enslavement? Are there clerical members of the church, of our church, who do not follow the sources of Christian life? Have they adapted to changing times? Do they ignore Christ's Gospel message and Christianity's founding message? Do they refuse to think with the church—the whole church? Do these, who wield power and authority, love each member personally or do they pay lip service to the fundamental questions of living the Christian life?

Finally, do they listen or do they enslave? Do they use their power in a healthy or an unhealthy way?

That is the question, you know.

It all boils down to how these clerics view the church and all organizations within it. Do they see Christians gathered around a center of communion and leadership, or do they see Christians ruled through a jurisdictional and organizational structure? Is their church essentially communal or juridical?

These questions underlie and underscore how the world sees the men and women of the church. But the caricature of the "boys' church/girls' church" has gone about as far as it can go. No matter where I travel, I am immediately asked: "What about the way the Vatican treats the nuns?" That is all anyone learns from major media. The question comes from believers and nonbelievers, from people of all faiths and of no faith.

Yet it is not necessarily "Vatican vs. nuns." Rather, it is a question of whether the church is primarily communal–involving everyone, or juridical–with restricted participation. Within one "side" of the apparent conflict are many clerics who identify more with the Vatican's juridical structure; within the other "side" are many others, especially women religious, whose organizations are governed communally.

Even deeper within each "side" are conflicted questions of what holds the church together, what brings each "side" to the table–indeed, whether members of each "side" will even sit at the table.

Yet they all profess to love the same God.

The Christian response to any difference is to sit and talk, to stay in deep conversation, to pray and think and talk some more. But the response of some clerics is to ignore the other, to shun the writer or speaker who pushes the conversation forward. But shunning is not a part of who we are as Christians. Shunning is done by the weak, not the strong. Shunning is done by the angry, not the peaceful. Shunning is done by people who may not fully understand their own positions and who therefore cannot address the positions of others.

The 800 sisters who attended the LCWR meeting in Nashville traveled back to their convents and monasteries. Some returned to apartments or houses. All returned to the charge they received from their own communities to govern with care and concern, to lead with insight and understanding, to live the Gospel in the light of their founding charisms. They are committed to respectful dialogue.

They are. They most certainly are.

A Letter
to a Woman Religious

Dear Betty,

The whole thing is a heartbreak. I can picture the tears you've shed, for your community, for your vocation, for your very life. Please believe me, nothing was wasted.

The noise that came from Rome about American women religious is in large part just that: the blustering of old men, translated into official-looking documents by cassock-clad junior clerics who wistfully wander the Curia's halls dreaming of a more orderly church, where lace is white and lay folk are quiet.

It might sound like an indictment of you, but the world heard it as an indictment of them. They want a tidy, controlled church. That's not likely to happen.

I think most of the 1.2 billion Catholics see the church differently. I think they see the church as communal and collegial, not collaborative and political. That is the big difference, you know. What scholars call "communion ecclesiology" looks at the church the way you do, just that, as a communion. What they call "juridical ecclesiology" is creeping more and more to the fore and creating the sort of top-down situation the church is in right now.

It wasn't always like this. Some scholars say the initial claim to papal primacy came in the late second century. That it was actually a good thing—a place and people to coordinate belief and practice. Over the centuries things evolved, until now Rome is—or at least we perceive it as—the absolute center of all power and authority in the church. That makes bishops into regional vice presidents, ever searching for the next rung up the ladder...to what?

That's the change I've noticed over the years since the Second Vatican Council closed its doors and the windows blew wide open. I barely remember the council and certainly was not aware of it at the time. That could help explain the nostalgic ones wishing for a dreamy past church. They've seen the old sepia and Kodachrome photos–the boys and girls lined up by Sister in her huge habit, Father with that little hat, the bishop in ermine with jewel-encrusted gloves.

You're 74, the average age, they tell me, of all the women religious in the United States. You were there in that photo. I guess from your perspective, the changes were very big. You rode them well. Now you're in the middle of it all with few sisters behind you and many more already gone to God. I saw on CBS the other day a segment saying that even your own name, Betty, is out of fashion–and the Midwest's "Betty Clubs" are dying out.

I know it hurts. I've said this to you before, probably 25 years ago. The drop in vocations to women's institutes is not because young women don't trust you. It is because they don't trust the men. It is a new world, as you well know, and very few women are willing to be treated the way the men–I guess by that, I mean Rome–have treated the Leadership Conference of Women Religious and, by extension, you.

I did read the document from the Congregation for the Doctrine of the Faith you sent around. Did you notice it is not numbered and it is not signed? It is on the congregation's letterhead, but on behalf of whom? And on behalf of what? Whoever wrote it seems to think of himself (and you can be sure it is "himself") as defender of the One True Faith, minion of the pope, and a future cardinal. Because I've read the LCWR materials as well, I see the Congregation's errors, both of fact and reasoning. The Vatican's paper was, in large respect, a sly attempt to sully the names of all of you. (Did I tell you already about the sister who came up to me at church the other day? She said, "Why don't they just burn all 57,000 of us at the stake and be done with it?")

It seems to be over, but it very well may not be. No matter. There is nothing you or I can do about it now. But there are still the poor, the imprisoned, the ill, the downtrodden, the hungry. I think your work–even though it's volunteer–down at the soup kitchen is what it is all about. And I hope your arthritis is doing better.

A New Spin?

As the stories spin and positions harden, the very real male-female divide in the Catholic Church grows and grows. It's now still very much bishops v. nuns. As Rodney King asked during the 1992 Los Angeles riots, "Can we all get along, can we call get along, can we stop making it horrible...we'll get our justice...let's try to work it out."

The poison in the stew now is the same as when Los Angeles erupted into flames then, enveloping the lives of real people. Media riot coverage incited more riots, thereby inciting more media coverage.

It's not much different in the church today. Public perceptions of internal church issues fill the public eye. The male-female teams and their issues line up. Bishops: anti-health care, anti-social service, anti-intellectual. Sisters: pro-health care, pro-social service, pro-intellectual.

So the bishops are beginning to notice the chinks in their vestments. One says they need help with "messaging;" another wants someone to "strategize." They broadcast their meetings—a study in black.

Meanwhile, the sisters keep their cool, offering occasional statements but few interviews. They hold board meetings by conference call. Their other meetings are relatively closed.

The bishops are losing, big time. Do they have any idea how much anger there is or how ridiculous the U.S. church looks to the world? Ordinary church-going folks, including (and especially) the grandmothers, are literally screaming in support of the church's women religious, while passing more than disrespectful comments about bishops, especially their own.

Why?

The church's sole message—that all human beings are made in the image and likeness of God and all deserve respect and protection—is being derailed by criticisms of the bishop—not the sisters—from within and without. And many of them are justified, from within and without.

In addition, the internal wars continue. Over at *National Review*, pundit George Weigel criticized events at the Catholic Theological Society of America's St. Louis meeting, which he did not attend. Weigel indicts the 400 theologians who tabled a resolution that used the flashpoint terms "religious liberty" and "mandate." Voting for or voting against that wording was more a political than theological decision. Either vote would drag the society into a public debate with admitted moral theological considerations. But full floor debate was impossible at the end of the Friday evening business meeting. I am certain of this. I was there.

Without question, the problem of forcing objecting employers to directly or indirectly pay for contraceptives, abortifacients, and sterilizations is a stone in the eye of the Catholic Church and its affiliated ministries. But exacerbating the internal church situation is not helping.

Catholics would best take Rodney King's advice to heart. And if the bishops want help with "messaging" and "strategizing," they might first take a look at what the women religious of the church have been doing.

IV. THE ABUSE OF WOMEN

Death over a Cup of Water?

Asia Bibi is still in jail. It's more than nuts. It's sick.

In 2009, this wife of a brick maker and mother of five went berry picking to earn an extra 250 Pakistani rupees near her simple home in Punjab. That would be about $2.50.

The end of the story: She has been sentenced to death for blaspheming against the Prophet Muhammad.

According to *Blasphemy*, a book co-written with French television journalist Anne-Isabelle Tollet that tells Asia's story, it started when she used a common cup to take water twice from a well in the berry field. Another woman shouted that Asia, a Christian, made the water *haram*, or unclean for Muslims.

All the other berry pickers were Muslim.

They say it was more than 100 degrees that day, so maybe the heat pushed the rage button on either side of the discussion. Perhaps Asia did not think of or did not know that detail of the laws of cleanliness. She was thirsty. She took two cups of water. And when confronted, she said to the accusers, "I think Jesus would see it differently from Muhammad."

Not the best comment to make on a hot June day to a crowd of angry women in the second-most-populous Muslim-majority country. There are almost 3 million Christians and almost 3 million Hindus in Pakistan. But the other 174 million people, or 97 percent of the population, are Muslim.

The confrontation by the well got nasty. They called Asia a filthy Christian and Jesus a bastard. They challenged her to convert to Islam. She countered, "I'm not going to convert. I believe in my religion and in Jesus Christ who died on the cross for the sins of mankind. What did your Prophet Mohammad ever do to save mankind? And why should it be me who converts instead of you?"

Then it got worse.

Somehow, Asia escaped alive, but five days later she went back to pick some berries and earn some rupees. A mob beat and dragged her to the law, which some months later found her guilty of blasphemy and sentenced her to death.

They say Asia is the only woman so sentenced in this century. She has been waiting in filthy prison cells for nearly six years now. On October 16, 2014, the Lahore High Court dismissed Noreen's appeal and upheld her death sentence. Her lawyers plan to appeal to the Supreme Court.

It's not that her situation has gone unnoticed. Pope Benedict spoke publicly on her behalf. France offered her political asylum. The United Nations has heard all about her.

"It is a bit like being an orphan in your own country," Asia Bibi said through a go-between to Tollet, who put *Blasphemy* together with Asia's own words. Tollet reported from Islamabad for three years until the book came out in French in 2011. An English translation appeared in the United Kingdom a year later. Now, a small Chicago publisher has it in paperback and for the Kindle.

There is a book. There are websites. There is even a petition. But nothing really has been done to save this simple woman, now in her early forties and suffering from a swollen foot in a stinking, windowless cell maybe five feet wide.

Before they moved her, Asia lived on food her husband brought. Now she takes the common prison meals, always fearing poison. There is a 5,000 euro bounty offered by a Muslim cleric to the one who kills her.

Did I mention how friendly the United States is with Pakistan? Since Asia Bibi's been in jail, the United States has sent more than $3.5 billion dollars in "civilian assistance." According to the U.S. Department of State, regular "security assistance"—interrupted during an eight-month spat—resumed not long ago. More recently, the United States picked up its "Strategic Dialogue with Pakistan in order to foster a deeper, broader, and more comprehensive partnership."

Maybe the United States can include Asia Bibi in their dialogue? What is the craziness that allows her situation?

She is not the only person—male or female; Christian, Hindu or Muslim—stuck in some Pakistani prison suffering because of real or imagined charges of blasphemy. The sharp edge of the law within that supposedly secular state cuts anyone in its path.

Disrespect for another's religious belief is a deeply serious affliction in any situation or society. Prejudices exist. Jobs and perquisites and preferential treatments can sway back and forth according to the beliefs of the powerful. That is the human condition. But six years of inhumane imprisonment for a simple woman is more than enough.

I think Jesus and Muhammad would see it exactly the same way.

Another Day, Another Rape

Half of India lacks bathrooms. In rural Uttar Pradesh, poor women use the same fields of sugar cane or mint that by day provide them work. Not long ago at bedtime, two teenaged girls went out and did not return. Their fathers found them the next morning, hanged by their head scarves from a mango tree.

Yes, they were dead. Of course, they had been raped.

Two hundred million persons live in their huge northern state of Uttar Pradesh. In the complexities of the caste-bound culture, the two Shakya girls were lower than the three young Yadav men who raped and murdered them. Uttar Pradesh is controlled by the Yadav.

Now there is great hue and cry, the people protest, the government declares an investigation. Two local constables, whom the victims' families say ignored their nighttime pleas for help, have also been arrested. These facts are new. Unfortunately, the storyline is not.

Rape is sport for some in India. Not long ago, three cousins tricked and trapped a 22-year-old nun in Odisha and raped her for a week. More recently, courts found five men guilty of gang raping a young photojournalist in Mumbai.

Yes, the church has said a word or two. One of Pope Francis' advisors, Cardinal Oswald Gracias, president of the

Catholic Bishops' Conference of India, named rape "physical and emotional terrorism." The bishops' conference called for a "change in attitude" toward women.

That is not enough. In fact, it is nearly nothing.

Memo to Cardinal Gracias:

Please state firmly and clearly that women are made in the image and likeness of God. Referencing and reverencing the Almighty will address the patchwork of religious beliefs across India. For the 24 million Christians among the 1.2 billion populace please state specifically and forcefully that women can image Christ. Your own website presents "India's shame: female genocide, aborted before birth, poisoned, drowned, stifled, deliberately neglected, burnt for dowry, sacrificed in childbirth, killed in sickness, and starved to death." Unless and until you teach the sacredness of all persons, nothing will change. It just won't.

Do you fear that if you say women can image Christ there will be huge numbers of women storming seminaries demanding to be priests? That does not seem quite likely in your culture but, even so, would that be so terrible? You know, of course, that women have and can again be deacons, ordained to minister *in persona Christi servi*. What do you care if theologians start jumping up and down about priesthood once women are returned to the diaconate? The church teaches it does not have the authority to ordain women as priests. Do you not believe that?

The choice is yours. In Rome, over at the Congregation for the Doctrine of the Faith, Cardinal Gerhard Müller says women cannot image Christ. That attitude is just too nasty to behold. It's not theology. It's misogyny. Not only that, it spawns the sickness underlying each and every disrespectful action toward a woman. You know exactly what I am talking about. Please use your influence on behalf of the women of India and of the world whose lives depend on Christian teachings being honestly taught. Until you do, nothing you say will have any merit.

It is really that bad in India. The stories melt into each other. Some are half-remembered or not recalled at all. Was it five men in New Delhi, and three girls in Bangalore? Or was it the other way around? Were they sentenced; did they go free? Are the girls dead, or are they living shunned by fellow villagers in a life of lonely poverty? Did I hear that one committed suicide? Or maybe that was in Pakistan or Yemen. Or was it Syria?

We know this particular outrage was in Uttar Pradesh, India, where the Taj Mahal and two other World Heritage Sites command millions of visitors each year. Uttar Pradesh is the state where Jawaharlal Nehru, India's first prime minister, was born. It was Nehru, in fact, who said India would not prosper until every house had a proper toilet. Nehru died in 1964. Indian women still fear the call of nature, and so much more.

Does Anybody Care about Human Trafficking?

The story is 20 years old, but it is true. Two Chinese girls came to the United States. Taken to a New Jersey motel, they were raped repeatedly and forced to work as prostitutes in New York City's Chinatown.

The girls were never left alone or allowed out of their apartment-brothel. They spoke no English, but they could watch television. Soon, they figured out that dialing 911 on the telephone would bring police. But where were they? A customer supplied the address. So on a slow afternoon, one girl gave their guard special favors while other dialed 911. Within minutes, a Chinese-speaking cop showed up. Game over.

That's just two Chinese girls in New York. The United Nations reports that at any given time 2.5 million trafficking victims fuel a $32 billion industry. Half are children. Most are younger than 24. For every 800 persons trafficked, there is but one conviction.

It is all over the world. It is not stopping. Small scale or large, the slave trade continues.

Not long ago in New York, Indian consulate official Devyani Khobragade, 39, was deported amidst charges she lied on work visa paperwork for a servant she paid $3.31 per hour. At least that victim was paid something. Many are not. And forced servitude is the least of it: Nearly half of trafficking victims—mostly women and girls—become sex slaves of one sort or another.

Whether it is an Indian diplomat in New York underpaying and overworking her servant or the sleazy element that provides prostitutes near sporting events and trade shows, the people who trade in human flesh have networks large and small to keep things going.

The heartbreak is that trafficking is growing, not declining, and those who should know better seem to wink and turn aside because, you know, boys will be boys. And it's the world's oldest profession. And the girls wouldn't be doing it anyway if they didn't like it. And it's private behavior and no one is getting hurt. And, didn't you see *The Wolf of Wall Street*?

The global moral collapse is not stopping. Yet another UN study will count the victims, but can it ever count the cost?

I think we can draw straight lines from the fact of genuinely gross movies about the exploitation of women suddenly becoming mainstream to unbridled anger at women exploding on the Internet to the basest disrespect of women (and many men) through human trafficking.

The real "trickle-down effect" is behavioral. Bad behavioral.

Too many men in this world have no respect for women.

When Pope Francis says women should be called to service, not servitude, his words can be applied to the cappa magna crowd as well as to the traffickers. In a very real sense, there is not much daylight between the ways some Catholic clergy look at women. I will never get one comment out of my head: "Ordaining a woman is the same as ordaining a lamp post or a cat." I heard that in a seminary classroom from a priest professor of sacramental theology. The obvious implication is that women are not fully human. The second shoe, of course, is that they cannot image Christ.

That is what Francis needs to fix. He's been asked to call a world day of prayer focused on the global cancer of human trafficking. Some Italian nuns suggested February 8, the feast day of St. Josephine Bakhita, the nineteenth-century African slave woman kidnapped as a child, who was so young she forgot her own name.

Bought and sold at least five times and then given away, when she was 19, Bakhita's owner left her caring for his young daughter at an Italian convent. When he returned, Bakhita refused to leave with him. Italian courts ruled in her favor, since slavery had been outlawed before her capture in both her Sudanese homeland and in Italy.

Bakhita is Arabic for "lucky." She got her freedom. But there is still a lot of trafficking in and through Sudan. There are still many employers who abuse their servants. There are hundreds, if not thousands, of persons trafficked every year from China. The trafficking sex trade still slithers along a highway or byway near you.

The solution begins with two questions: What does it mean to be human? And what does it mean to care?

V. MEN AND WOMEN

Humanity for All:
A Pastoral Letter on Men
(first draft)

Brothers and Sisters in Christ:

1. Men are called to follow our Lord Jesus Christ and proclaim his Gospel in the midst of a complex world. This reality poses both opportunities and difficulties. Men must be measured by how they protect or undermine the dignity of all persons. Their decisions have consequences and moral content; they help or hurt people, strengthen or weaken family life, advance or diminish the quality of justice in our land. Yet many men do not understand what it is to be human. They do not know who they are.

2. This is why we have written *Humanity for All: A Pastoral Letter on Men*. This letter is a personal invitation to men to use the resources of our faith to shape their lives so that they better protect their own dignity and basic rights as well as the dignity and basic rights of women, both in this land and around the world.

3. The pastoral letter has been a work of careful inquiry, wide consultation, and prayerful discernment. We offer this

pastoral message to and for men in the hope they will live their faith in the marketplace and at home as truly human persons, rejecting the temptation to be defined by violence, substance abuse, and the misplaced idols of sports, politics, and media.

4. We specifically write for men who respond violently to society in general and to women in particular. We recognize that the largest cohort of imprisoned persons are male, many of whom have succumbed to a culture that idolizes weapons, wealth, and power. We offer the suggestion that men's idolatry of these often become a cause of inappropriate sexual activity. Such is of particular concern and is connected to increases in human trafficking and spousal abuse, as well as to increases in depression and substance addictions, especially alcoholism.

5. We note that while the majority of men do not evidence outward signs of emotional disturbance, many suffer from an immaturity that causes them to believe they are superior to women. Part of these difficulties stem from familial issues of shame and relationships with parents. Other root causes include inabilities to measure up to so-called "masculine" roles as defined by cinema and other entertainment vehicles, certain sports games, and clericalism in some parts of our church. This latter difficulty is exacerbated by uncontrolled access to the media of communication by certain clerics who seek to undermine the enriching influences of the Second Vatican Council.

6. Today is a time of challenge for men as each day more barriers arise against the recognition of the equality of women before God. We urge the men of the church to work assiduously

to deflate all stereotypes for persons of both genders. We recognize that "equal" does not mean "the same," yet we urge all persons to work to open more doors to cooperative ministries between men and women.

7. We know that lay persons value the recognition that they are vital forces in the world. Those who feel valued and who genuinely are respected embrace the expanded roles given to them since Vatican II. They bring knowledge, education, skills, and leadership to both society and the church. May the men of the church see and accept these gifts, particularly in women.

8. We write this pastoral letter to share our hopes for the dialogue and action it might generate. Our prayers are directed at strengthening the hope of women whose liberty and equality have been taken from them by men who have forgotten or who have never known their own humanity. May our faith and our concern spur all persons to individual and collective recognition of the humanity of all persons for the transformation of the church and of the world.

What Catholic Women Do

If it were not for Mary Magdalene, we never would have heard about the Resurrection. The men would still be in the Upper Room, trying to figure how to get out of town.

Do you sometimes wonder if things have changed?

I don't think they have.

Men are careful. Men are circumspect. Men, after all, have their careers to consider.

Women just do it.

That could be a reason Jesus did not name women as Apostles, or at least why the women who were there did not bother with the title. The women were not interested in advancement or having their names remembered. They were simply doing.

What did the men want? Power? Authority? They preached the message, it is true, but they also jockeyed with each other for position. And who could forget the one who sold out for cash?

So, have things changed? Few will argue with the statement that the men have made a mess of things.

Of course, the Big Events go forward. The pope goes here. The pope goes there. The symbolism is striking. On the one hand, it seems insane. On the other, it is important, it really is.

But it is also very, very important, for Christians—a third of the world—to keep an eye on the empty tomb. Christ is risen, that tomb proclaims. Christ has died, Christ is risen, Christ will come again. That is what really makes a difference.

The women just keep on keeping on. They fold their sorrows and hurts into their hearts and carry on. The women live the lives and do the work that keeps the world spinning. They are the teachers and the shopkeepers; the doctors and the homemakers. The women are the managers and the bus drivers and the librarians. They are the backbone of the parish, of the community, of the family. Some—maybe more than some—are infected with a greed for power and authority. But more than some have both power and authority and wear them lightly, wield them gracefully.

Meanwhile, Important Things and Big Events will come and go. Power and authority will rise and they will fall. People will be hurt, terribly, and some will die.

The women, meanwhile, will keep announcing the Resurrection.

Political Platforms

I'm tired of the arguing, the truth-shading, the smirking and the jokes. I'm tired of it all. Here are the seven issues I want addressed starting today, this minute. Not tomorrow. Not next week. Not after whatever election is on the horizon. Today, please.

Feed the hungry:
Hunger is the first pain of poverty. Interlaced economies are both substance and cause of the poverty spreading more in the Third World than in the genteel First. Individuals, families, whole villages are chronically exhausted for want of food. These are real malnourished people, suffering especially a lack of protein. Some statisticians count 925 million hungry people among the more than 7 billion hanging on to the planet. In the U.S. alone, almost 47 million people are on food stamps—government credit card aid that neither lessens the embarrassment at the check-out nor covers the entire grocery cart.

Give drink to the thirsty:
The world is rapidly losing its water supply, without which we shrivel and die. All of us. Water is the new oil. If you control

the water, you control the ability to grow crops, to move goods and supplies, to create power. World leaders know water is a strategic and economic resource; more than 260 river basins are shared by two or more countries, and they don't always get along. There's been a tiff going on for years between Brazil and Paraguay over the Itaipu Dam. While individuals and corporations roam the world buying water rights, more than a billion people lack access to safe drinking water. Pollution is rampant and is killing the seas, especially the microscopic life that begins the oceanic food chain.

Clothe the naked:
It used to be a teenage ritual to sneak a look at the feathered, painted, semi-naked bodies in *National Geographic*. Now photographers document naked little ones, men in rags, women in less. They have no clothes. They have no shoes. While the polished wealthy of the world shop on Rome's Via Veneto or Los Angeles' Rodeo Drive (the World Bank says Americans spend $50 billion annually on shoes alone), as many as 300 million children go barefoot, each one prey to injury and disease.

Shelter the homeless:
The world's political systems practically conspire to create refugees. Displaced persons trek from Somalia to Kenya, from South Sudan to North Sudan. They leave Afghanistan, Sierra Leone, Myanmar, and the Palestinian Territories. People in richer nations are little better off. As housing booms became

housing busts, broken people removed the "better life" signs from their doors and slipped away. In Spain, in Ireland, in the United States, wherever a mortgage broker made a euro or a dollar on a family's hopes, people wonder why their dreams evaporated.

Visit the sick:
Health care is a worldwide mangled mess. Poor countries have few doctors, with less equipment and supplies. Rich countries have highly trained and specialized physicians who send as much as a quarter of their incomes to insurance companies. Hospitals go broke. Nursing homes are engulfed in scandals. In between are millions of people with colds, injuries, and chronic conditions. Many can pay their bills through private or government programs. Many more cannot.

Ransom the captive:
Too many women are subject to denigrating, humiliating conditions. In too many places, they are not allowed education. They cannot vote. They are not permitted to drive a car. In the macho world, they are regarded as baby-making factories, good only for pleasure and production. Even in civilized nations, including those with women at the helms of government and education, the stiff undercurrent of old-boy chatter blocks advancement (or even entry) into halls of power, be they private, civic, or religious.

Bury the dead:
At least the world usually buries the people its wars, mayhem, and negligence kill daily. But other lives are ended purposefully without a passing thought. The roadkill of the so-called civilized world includes the abortions it supports for emotional or financial convenience, without a nod to the scientific understanding that this is a human being. (That is, in fact, the biological term.) We do not know at what point that life becomes a "person." But we know for sure the conceptus would become one, not a frog.

Dear political leaders, please figure it out. More wealth might help: the wealth that spills into jobs, generating goods, services, and taxes. I know taxes are a tricky business. Too many taxes discourage new businesses and shrink jobs. Too few taxes endanger the infrastructure new businesses depend on, and folks need to get to work.

The back-and-forth and back-and-forth about the economy has never really addressed the creation of wealth. But without work and a way to get there, people cannot get food, water, clothing, shelter, and health care. Human dignity and respect for themselves and all creation evaporates.

I want you—whether you are a candidate, president, bishop, king or dictator—to take a long hard look at your dinner table tonight and think about those hungry, thirsty, naked, homeless people. I want you to think about their rights and dignity as persons. I want you to understand how human flesh and blood suffers.

And I want you to figure it out.

VI. THE HIERARCHY

Planet Vatican

You don't have to speak Italian to understand the Vatican's recent "Women's Cultures" events, but it could help. (It was all in Italian.)

The Pontifical Council for Culture touted its meetings as analyses of the status of the world's 3.5 billion women. (About 43 million of them speak Italian.)

The council's offensive Christmas-week infomercial was supposed to crowdsource a video for its opening event, which did flash a few (unreadable) submissions toward its end. The *avant garde* production in Teatro Argentina, a Roman opera house, included a jazz trio, professionally produced videos, and scripted declamations. (All in Italian.)

What are we to make of all this? The Pontifical Council for Culture seems to be the Vatican's faculty of arts and letters. Like all Vatican councils and congregations, it is predominantly male. It includes 13 cardinals, 14 bishops and four "men of culture." It has 35 consultors, including seven women. Its 16-person staff has male professionals and four female secretaries. It is headed by four clerics: a prefect, a delegate, a secretary, and an undersecretary. Such is the crowd that set out to advise the pope on women. (In Italian.)

The statistics are important. The council's erudite

president, 72-year-old biblical scholar Cardinal Gianfranco Ravasi, put together a group of female advisers (all Italian but one) to create a working document and a presentation for the full council's meeting. The document's website included a photograph of a woman's headless torso bound in ropes, "art" by the bondage aficionado Man Ray.

The written materials are pretty disturbing, too. Did you ever see a Vatican document without footnotes? The paper belies its content—equality and difference, generativity, the female body, and women in the church—and the overall impression is quite serious: Women don't cite facts.

Let's focus on one statement in the working document: "There is no discussion here of women priests, which according to statistics is not something that women want."

You read that correctly. Forget the fact of multiple women's ordination organizations and of the worldwide Roman Catholic Womenpriests movement. Forget the fact that, according to the Center for Applied Research in the Apostolate at Georgetown University, there are 13,219 women (58 percent of the total) in Catholic ministerial studies in the United States. Forget the fact that, according to the Pittsburgh-based Association of Theological Schools, there are 181 women studying for the professional Master of Divinity degree in its 52 Catholic member seminaries. Forget the fact that, at least according to a small sampling of nondenominational Christian seminaries, more than half their Catholic M.Div. students are female. In fact, statistics demonstrate that nearly 60 percent of Catholics in ministerial studies in the United States are female.

So again, according to the working document: "There is no discussion here of women priests, which according to statistics is not something that women want."

What statistics?

We know what the church teaches about women priests. But at the end of their meeting, when the pope spoke to the group, he again called for a more widespread and incisive presence of women in the church. Did they expect that? Did they hear that?

What, exactly, did they talk about in the sessions on women in the church?

The proceedings of the council's few days of meetings are unpublished so far, but its interventions on church came only from Anne-Marie Pelletier, the first woman to win the Ratzinger Prize, Sr. Mary Melone, rector of the Pontifical Antonianum University, and Lucetta Scaraffia, a relatively outspoken supporter of women's causes—within limits. Did their papers—no doubt delivered in Italian—represent the other 3.5 billion women on Earth?

Back at the sparsely attended opening event at the 700-seat Teatro Argentina, the final words were from St. Catherine of Siena, a patroness of Italy and of Europe. They quoted Catherine as writing: "If you are what you should be, you will set fire to the entire world."

That is not what Catherine wrote in Letter T368. What she wrote was: "If you are what you should be, you will set fire to all of Italy."

Italy is not the entire world. But that was the perspective, start to finish.

We must ask: What about the rest of the planet?

The Twilight Zone

Narrator: There is a fifth dimension beyond that known to man. It is a dimension as vast as space and as timeless as infinity. It is the middle ground between light and shadow, between science and superstition, and it lies between the pit of man's fears and the summit of his knowledge. This is the dimension of imagination. It is an area we call the Twilight Zone.

Female presenter (off): Other people call it the Roman Catholic Church.

(Fade to red and black)

We could go on with the script, but it is too predictable. OK, it's not the whole church, but there is most definitely a Twilight Zone out there, and it is growing.

Imagine, if you will, the discussion in the Pontifical Council for Culture about the Man Ray bondage sculpture it used as a logo for meetings about women:

He: It was presented by an expert and it shows the way women are in society.

She: Are you kidding? Did you miss the fact that today's largest-grossing movie is the bondage jamboree "Fifty Shades of Grey"?

He: We are keeping it.

(Fade to black and blue)

The council's cardinal president really did defend using that illustration. He really did refuse to remove it. He also brushed aside complaints about the council's airhead infomercial asking for one-minute videos about women's lives.

Explanation: Complaints only came from the United States and Canada.

Translation: Ignore those uppity North Americans.

No kidding. A well-educated Roman Catholic cardinal defended the insults he presided over. Worse, he does not understand the insults. He simply does not get it.

He is not alone. The alternative Catholic dimension is beyond anything you know in space and time. It exists in the minds of too many new clerics bounding out of seminaries, birettas in hand, ready to straighten out the mess caused by taking women seriously. You know: all this business about women being equal to men, even working as professionals (gasp!) outside the home!

Give me, as they say, a break.

Everybody's talking about it. No one is doing anything about it. The pope has warned against poorly formed priests and clerical careerists. Yet the wave against normalcy continues. Who is minding the chancery?

More to the point: What are they teaching in seminaries about women, about sex and sexuality?

Do they prefer shadow to light? Do they speak more

from fear than from knowledge? Do they teach more with superstition than with science?

Consider, if you will, the San Francisco pastor who banned female altar servers in his downtown parish. His associate priest handed out a confession "guide" to schoolchildren too young to pronounce—or understand—words like "sodomy" and "masturbation."

Consider as well in your attempt to understand where these priests are coming from the report in Commonweal magazine from a young man who left seminary with vivid memories of strange discussions about sex, sexuality, and women.

Finally, consider the fact that priests still get away with jokes about single women and about mothers-in-law before they prattle away at their unprepared homilies.

There is too much of this stupidity going around, too much fear of women, and too much ignorance, misinformation, and childishness.

The People of God deserve so much more.

Even so, the future of this Twilight Zone is assured. The lace warriors use all manner of social media. A legion of blogger-priests paints the Internet 50 shades of red, whining about altar servers and chapel veils while not so secretly wishing for a closet filled with silk brocade vestments. Their followers staunchly defend…what? What? What?

Christians everywhere are moving through life gently, turning away from sin and toward the Gospel. But the bureaucracy chugs along in its own dimension, ignoring the retrograde backdrop, unknowing of the ways ignorant clericalism crushes the hearts and minds of women looking for the truth.

That bureaucracy does not know Christ. That bureaucracy does not know itself. If it did, if that bureaucracy knew Christ, and if that bureaucracy knew itself, it would not be in the Twilight Zone. Nor would it be so murderously cruel to women.

The Red and the Black

The Catholic roulette wheel keeps spinning long after the white smoke, the white cassock, and the white pallium appear. Even though the new pope is at the center, cardinals in red and black still surround him. Insider horse trading and old-school thinking remain. You may think the new pope is a surprise reformer, but you can't win big putting chips on double zero. Only American-style roulette has that bet.

While American-style journalism has been driving the news coming from Rome, American-style management and transparency will be a hard sell, even in the new papacy. No matter the qualifications of the latest man to climb into Peter's chair, the Vatican bank and overall curial messes will surely take up enough time and energy to hold up any reforms, even reforms requested by both sides of the marbled aisle.

Of course, the elephant in the Sistine Chapel is female, and she's not leaving. The general consensus from the sidelines is that women in authority would have cleaned up the mess of the sex abuse scandals more quickly and cleanly.

So now the men in red and black say they want to ameliorate women, but will they? Can they? It is entirely possible—even probable—they've figured out who keeps the family checkbook. Women are, to put it mildly, hopping mad at what has been going on, and they are keeping those checkbooks at home. So the latest wisdom is that women should have more power in the church.

Of course there is that little question of ordination. No orders, no office. No office, no authority. It is as simple (and as complicated) as that. You have to be a cleric to hold any real authority in the church, and you have to be ordained in order to become a cleric.

Don't hold your breath waiting for women priests. It's not going to happen.

But there are two ways around the problem, each reported in *The Tablet* in England. One, promoted by German Cardinal Walter Kasper, a Curia member for more than 10 years, would be to bless a fourth, non-ordained order of "deaconesses." Kasper would probably support a legal change allowing "deaconesses" to be clerics. The other answer comes from German Cardinal Karl Lehmann, a diocesan bishop for 30 years and a longtime supporter of women as deacons. Lehmann said the question of ordaining women to the diaconate has been around too long and it is time for "a binding and good decision."

Lehmann understands the problem. Kasper misses the elephant.

The fact is, they can't say "no," and they don't want to say "yes."

There is nothing new about ordaining women as deacons. Reportedly responding to Pope Paul VI's question in 1974, International Theological Commission member Cipriano

Vagaggini wrote that what the church has done, the church can do again. His treatise—in Italian—parses the ordination rituals of the early church and comes down clearly on the side of returning women to the one order of deacon. That is, scholarship argues not for some second-class "deaconess" status but rather for women in the ordained diaconate.

But the International Theological Commission found a way to ignore Vagaggini's (and others') recommendations, publishing an inconclusive document in 2002. The question seems to rest in Rome: "It pertains to the ministry of discernment which the Lord established in his Church to pronounce authoritatively on this question."

But who does the discerning? Does the Curia stop the spinning wheel, or do the 1.2 billion Catholics have any say in the matter? Are the men in red and black the representatives of the church, or do they represent the inside of that spinning wheel? Will Pope Francis be able to get past the markers to an old answer for a new age that includes governance and ministry by women?

The top line inside bet pays out the best on every roulette wheel. It is obvious what the church needs. But will the red and the black and the new white take the chance?

Getting the Message?

Pope Francis has made it pretty clear: He wants more women involved in things churchy. That might even include listening to what women have to say. You think?

Two prelates seem to have gotten the memo.

In Ireland, the diocesan bishop of Killaloe, Kieran O'Reilly, canceled his plans to introduce only half (the male half) of the ancient ministry of the diaconate following objections from his lay ministers and many others from outside the diocese. Meanwhile, in Rome, Cardinal Gerhard Müller, prefect of the Congregation for the Doctrine of the Faith, had his slate of five women approved for the reconfigured International Theological Commission (ITC).

Are things are looking up? Will women's voices echo within episcopal palaces and curial hallways? Maybe.

The Irish situation may be an example of a bishop finally getting it. With about 100 priests for his relatively large diocese—which cuts across Ireland from the Atlantic seaboard in county Clare through Limerick, Tipperary and Offaly to Laois, nearly at the other end of the island—O'Reilly thought deacons were a great idea. His pastoral letter listed all the things deacons could do. The problem? Most of the tasks are already taken up by lay ministers. That would be female lay minsters.

So the women could still do the work, but the men would be preaching and baptizing and marrying.

It took about a day for the women to get organized. Their complaint was simple: Why add a clerical layer between the priest and the lay ministers, especially when the bishop's own pastoral plan promised to "empower men and women"? So within a few weeks of announcing his wish for the male-only diaconate in Killaloe, the bishop backtracked and announced its suspension.

Good news? Maybe.

Meanwhile, over at the doctrinal congregation, they're getting ready for the five women named to the ITC, which Pope Paul VI created 45 years ago, when he formally sought advice from many of the stars of the Second Vatican Council. The lineup then included Passionist Barnabas Ahern; Oratorian Louis Bouyer; Dominican Yves Congar; Benedictine Cipriano Vagaggini; Jesuits Walter Burghardt, Bernard Lonergan, Henri de Lubac, and Karl Rahner; one ex-Jesuit, Hans Urs von Balthasar; 20 others; and Joseph Ratzinger.

Pope Francis did say he wanted more women in positions of responsibility: His exact words were a "more incisive feminine presence in the church" in his interview with Jesuit editor Antonio Spadaro. Francis has used the word "incisive" again, more than once.

Every five years, the ITC replaces a few members. Ten years ago, the first two women joined. Now, five women and 25 men make up the body. So it looks like Müller got the memo.

Or did he?

The women appointed at Müller's request seem to be from the most conservative edges of theology and philosophy. Aside from Sr. Alenka Arko of the Loyola Community in the Russian Federation-Slovenia, about whom little can be found, the others are safe bets to support Müller's outlook toward women:

- Tracey Rowland, dean of the John Paul II Institute for Family and Marriage in Melbourne, Australia, and author of six books on Ratzinger;
- Marianne Schlosser, a professor of spirituality at the University of Vienna, who has written on consecrated virginity and contributed to works on Ratzinger;
- Moira McQueen, director of the Canadian Catholic Bioethics Institute;
- Mercy Sr. Prudence Allen, from Alma, Michigan, a former Denver seminary philosophy professor now at Lancaster University in England and completing her impressive study on the philosophical concept of woman from 750 B.C. to modern times.

The writings of at least four of the five draw straight lines from John Paul II to Benedict XVI in every issue that affects women. It is probably a safe bet that they agree with Müller that women cannot be ordained—as priests or deacons—because women cannot image Christ. It is an even safer bet that they have or will find arguments to support church teachings on any of the neuralgic social issues of the day, from the nature of homosexual relations to birth control and back again. Just in case they are not up-to-date on what other women theologians—particularly American women theologians—are up to, former U.S. Conference of Catholic Bishops' doctrine czar Capuchin Thomas Weinandy has been added to the ITC mix.

So no deacons in Killaloe, and five women on the ITC. Good news? Bad news? Who can say?

VII. POPE FRANCIS

Block That Metaphor

Pope Francis hurled an annoying—even insulting—metaphor at half the planet when, in a speech before the European Parliament, he likened Europe to a "haggard" grandmother "no longer fertile and vibrant." Not sure how many grandmothers he knows, but it's pretty clear he hasn't been to the gym lately. He might meet a few vibrant older women there.

OK, stand by, before we all get run over by the Francis Fan Club. He's terrific. He really is. He regularly says and does the right thing at the right time. Yet he seems to have a blind spot when it comes to women.

And it might not be entirely his fault.

Francis does not seem to have anyone coordinating his message. There is no way a professional advisor in the twenty-first century would allow the chief executive of any corporation to use demeaning metaphors about women. Yet this "selfie" shows Francis with his foot in his mouth.

As too many people have noticed, even though Francis talks a good game, he has done little for the women of the church. On the one hand he says, "There are still too many situations in which human beings are treated as objects… and who can then be discarded when no longer useful, due to weakness, illness or old age."

That would be from Francis's European Parliament "grandmother" speech. He was talking about society in general, but that would also be a direct description of the way the official church seems to view women: as baby-making machines, useless when "no longer fertile and vibrant." Don't believe that? Think about all the Catholic jokes about large families.

I am not complaining about Catholic doctrine here. I am merely pointing out the fact that the Vatican is about a century behind in knowing how to spread the central message of the Gospel. If Francis wants to change the world so that all persons are respected for their human dignity, so that all persons are seen as the image and likeness of God, he needs to include Catholic female human beings in the mix.

It does not look as if it will happen anytime soon. Even collapsing a few minor Vatican offices into some bureau for the laity with a woman at its head will not erase the general perception that Catholic women are not even at the low end of the totem pole. They're simply not on it.

Men know this. Women know this. Substitute the word "women" for "Europe" in the pope's speech and ponder how every woman is "...feeling less and less a protagonist in a world which frequently regards [her] with aloofness, mistrust and even, at times, suspicion." Every woman has suffered the bruising aloofness and mistrust and suspicion of men—especially clerics—well-taught that women are dangerous to their lives and livelihoods. Good Catholic women are virgins or mothers, period. And huge cadres of men see women who are not easily put into one of these two boxes as either temptresses or troublemakers.

The cavernous gap between what the church says and the way it appears to regard women is where the empty rhetoric falls into oblivion. Even the only American member of Francis's new Council of Cardinals fumbled on about how "men cannot be mothers" when the U.S. television program *60 Minutes* asked him about women in the church.

Francis said: "[T]he promotion of human rights is central…to advance the dignity of the person." How about promoting the human rights the church does not want to talk about? How about promoting the human rights of women, of all women, in ways both real and symbolic? Go ahead, use the "O" word (that would be "ordination"). Speak coherently about sacramental symbolism. Proclaim that women can indeed image Christ.

The pope said a while back: "[T]he feminine presence in the church has not fully emerged, because the temptation of machismo has not left space to make visible the role women are entitled to within the community." Where is that space? As Francis said about Europe, in the church great ideas seem to have lost their attraction, "…only to be replaced by the bureaucratic technicalities of its institutions."

That is quite true. The church, unable to block its metaphors, has blindsided itself and is stalling for time with its own technical fouls. But the clock is running out.

What the Pope Faces

Francis. Folks can't get enough of him. He's on the cover of *Time*, *The New Yorker*, and even *The Advocate*. But he's still an elderly Latin American male. Will he ultimately do anything for the women of the church and of the world?

Francis quite obviously sees the image of Christ in every person. He has complained that everything he hears about women is tainted by an "ideology of machismo." He even said—more than once—there should be a more "incisive" female presence in the church.

Yet he seems hamstrung by the machismo he complains about. What's going on?

I'm not so sure it's all his fault. First off, no matter what Francis says or does, the Vatican is not a female-friendly place. In an era of images, the photos tell the story. When the pope celebrates Mass in Santa Marta, a barrier reef of clerics stands between him and any woman. When he sends minions to invite the poor to his birthday breakfast, they bring back four homeless men. There are precious few photos of Francis with adult women.

A while back, the pope's Jesuit spokesman said the idea of women cardinals was "nonsense." Now the pope has agreed, calling women cardinals *"una battuta"*—a joke.

Is he skating on thin Italian ice?

Francis is unquestionably the world's pastor. Christians of every stripe are agog at his embodiment of the Gospel message. But he lives and works in an all-male society with all-male managers of the billion-person enterprise of the Catholic Church. That he is of Italian descent and from Argentina may not help.

Or might it? American feminism, where it takes a sharp left turn, often becomes harsh and anti-male—almost masculine—the kind of "machismo in skirts" the pope complained about. But as writer Camille Paglia points out, in many other countries, in "France, Italy, Spain, Latin America, and Brazil...professional women seem to have found a formula for asserting power and authority in the workplace while still projecting sexual allure and even glamour."

Which might be the problem. I think Francis can accept professional women. But can the celibate male organization he heads deal on an equal basis with women who assert power and authority in the workplace, not to mention project their sexual allure and glamour in the process?

Think not? Then that might be how the concept of women cardinals became "a joke." Science tells us women in red are very sexy, and in Italy a woman in red is often considered vulgar. Has the idea of a woman cardinal been overrun by low-level humor, developed to forestall real reform of the Curia and of the church?

Francis dismissed women cardinals, saying women should be valued and not "clericalized." I'm not so sure he was complaining about women cardinals so much as he was complaining about clericalism. The next day, clericalism turned up in his daily homily. He said a lack of prophecy in the church creates an emptiness that is filled by clericalism.

The lace and the *cappa magna* may be on the way out, but clericalism may still be on the trail of prophecy. Francis has said women must have a "more incisive presence in the church." But for a while that crucial sentence was missing on the Vatican website. It seems the Vatican posted the original *America* magazine translation, which dropped Francis' call for women's "more incisive presence in the church" and which now in book form uses the milder "stronger presence" for women in the church.

There are two very important points here: 1) The Vatican has posted an incomplete translation, and 2) nobody seems to have noticed notice or cared.

Or maybe they have noticed and maybe they do care. I still think Francis is the good guy in this scenario. But he cannot control everything, and image management can be a blood sport.

The Wrong Kind
of Papal "Ribbing"

I'm sure Pope Francis did not mean to insult half the human race, but in his first-ever interview with a woman journalist he "joked" that women are taken from Adam's rib and that women have power as rectory housekeepers.

OK, so he's old, he's tired, and he's got a million things on his mind. But, hello, Holy Father—the world is watching.

Franca Giansoldati, Vatican correspondent for the Rome daily newspaper *Il Messaggero*, asked the pope about women in the church. At first, he gave what seems to be his stock reply: Women are beautiful, "church" is a feminine word, we cannot do theology without femininity, we should work more on a theology of women.

She responded: "Don't you see a certain underlying misogyny?"

Francis replied: "The fact is, woman was taken from a rib." Giansoldati reports Francis laughed heartily as he called his comment a joke—*"una battuta"*—the same word he used months before to characterize the idea of women cardinals. Continuing, the pope agreed that "we" should go deeper into the issue of women, because without doing so "we" cannot understand the church itself.

Ignoring the insult, Giansoldati asked whether to "expect from you historic decisions, such as a woman department head, I am not saying of the Congregation for the Clergy...."

To which the pope continued his "ribbing": "Well, priests often come under the authority of the housekeeper."

What a riot.

Where to start? I can't help but wonder whether rectory housekeepers are root or result of clerical tone-deafness. I cannot believe that a world-class person like Francis, who seems so much in touch with individuals and their suffering, is capable of making remarks such as these. Yet I know he lives in a society where the ordinary needs of clerics are often taken care of by unmarried women or religious sisters who cook, clean, do laundry, order supplies, and serve as receptionists, often on nights and weekends. Just like Mom.

That still seems to be the case in much of the clerical world. Do an Internet search for "rectory housekeeper" and you will find job descriptions from coast to coast. Even new rectories have a room with a bath or a suite just off the kitchen or laundry room for the woman who runs the rectory household and, if Francis is to be believed, the priests.

Sometimes it's a little more than that. From my school days, I recall a housekeeper who followed the pastor to each new assignment. They finally got married when I was in graduate school.

Now, I know Francis is a religious and that he lived simply and did his own cooking back in Argentina. I know he does not live like King of the Vatican. I know he objects to high-living clerics. Yet his comment about housekeepers ruling the priests must come from someplace deep within the clerical society to which he belongs.

Unfortunately, remarks like his are not all that unusual.

When you catch some priests or bishops making similar comments, they chuckle, "Oh, no, ha ha, just joking." Other clerics, the ones who buy their own groceries and cook their own chicken, may smile wanly and say nothing when such wisecracks fly past. Only a very few will man up to the fact that these words hurled in jest have insulted a woman, thereby all women, thereby half the body of Christ.

That, after all, is the bottom line. The men who think like this just don't get it. Will they ever? How can the church move forward when the "we" is all male and women are the "they" to be both ridiculed and theologized about?

What the Holy Father Said

So, am I the only person on the planet who thinks Pope Francis said "yes" to women as deacons? The question was about what concrete measures the church should take, "for instance, the female diaconate or a woman at the head of a dicastery?"

No matter that there was a little Rome-speak in his answer. I am pretty sure he said "yes" to ordaining women as deacons.

The question came in Italian from *Le Figaro* religion editor Jean-Marie Guénois and also on behalf of a colleague from the French Catholic newspaper *La Croix*. Guénois spoke directly: "You said that the church without women loses its fruitfulness." And then Guénois asked about women as deacons and about women heading major portions of the church's bureaucracy.

Media reports burst with analysis of Francis' "who am I to judge" comment made on that plane ride from Rio in 2013. But a complete English translation of Francis's mostly Italian 80-minute chat with reporters on the aircraft is posted by the highly conservative Catholic News Agency (CNA). An outgrowth of the Peru-based *ACI Prensa*, "the largest and most visited web-provider of Catholic news in Spanish and Portuguese," CNA gives free access to Catholic entities. Its aim is to proselytize while it informs. It ran the transcript. It did not seem to focus on *Le Figaro's* question about women as deacons or the pope's apparently positive answer.

Nor did anyone else. Most news outlets at the time were falling over each other, racing to move the pope's comments about "gay persons"—his term. News flash: the pope reiterated Catholic teaching, both about homosexual activity and about the ordination of women as priests.

But the pope did not rule out—nor has any church teaching ruled out—the restoration of women to the ordained order of deacon. In fact, he led right into the current international discussion about women in the diaconate.

And, if the pope has reasserted that women cannot be ordained priests, then what is the problem? The fear of the naysayers to this obvious way to admit women to positions ordinarily—often legally—held only by clerics is that women as deacons portend women as priests. Such, of course, is a red herring. The church has stated (more or less definitively, depending on whose analysis you side with) that women cannot be priests.

But there is ample theological argumentation and historical evidence—Eastern and Western—that women have been and can again be ordained as deacons. In fact, the real problem about including women in ordained ministry is the lens through which the governing church (the men) sees the working church (the women), and that point was not lost on anyone.

Significant whining came from the bloggers and pundits

about Francis's use of the term "a theology of the woman." Most stated the obvious: Your Holiness, women are people, too. Theological anthropology fully covers both halves of the church.

Of course, the critics argued that the pope did not include women in the church's theological anthropology. I am sure he did not mean it to come out that way. For him, I think, the church needs to include women within the fuller understandings of theological anthropology. For him, I think, women are made in the image and likeness of God.

With or without what he called "a profound theology of the woman" Francis most assuredly said that the church needs women. He said, directly, that "the role of the woman in the church must not only end as mom, worker, limited. No! It's something else.... I think that we need to move further ahead in the development of this role and charism of the woman."

Francis continued, "I think that we haven't yet come up with a deep theology of the woman in the church. [She can] only do this, only do that. Now she is an altar server, now she reads the readings, she is the president of Caritas.... But there is more! We need to make a profound theology of the woman. This is what I think."

Thank you, Pope Francis. And, thank you Jean-Marie Guénois.

As American poet E.E. Cummings once wrote: "Always the beautiful answer who asks a more beautiful question."

About the Author

PHYLLIS ZAGANO, Ph.D., is senior research associate-in-residence and adjunct professor of religion at Hofstra University, Hempstead, New York, where she continues her research on women in the Catholic Churches (twenty-two Eastern and one Western). Author of many award-winning books and refereed articles in academic journals around the world, she speaks widely on women in ministry. She has received awards from the Religion Newswriters Association and the Catholic Press Association for her columns, and has been honored with the Isaac Hecker Award for Social Justice from Paulist Center (Boston) and the Saint Catherine of Siena Distinguished Lay Person Award from Voice of the Faithful.

Also Available from ACTA Publications

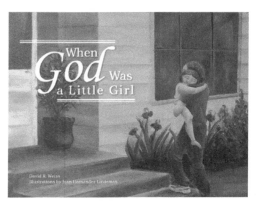

This beautifully-illustrated tale sparkles with the exuberant joy of God's creative energy revealed through the metaphor of a little girl doing an art project. Girls, whose outer appearance varies in age and culture throughout the book, mirror the uncontainable Love with which God sang the world into being. (32 pages, hardcover)

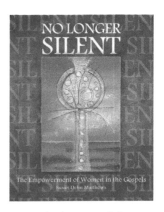

Susan Dehn Matthews creates a back story of the women who often have been overlooked in the Gospels, including Elizabeth, Mary of Nazareth, the sisters of Lazarus, Joanna, and Mary Magdalene. (256 pages, paperback)